SEEING EYE

CHRIS CONSIDINE

Cinnamon Press
:: small miracles from distinctive voices ::

Published by Cinnamon Press
Meirion House
Tanygrisiau
Blaenau Ffestiniog
Gwynedd, LL41 3SU
www.cinnamonpress.com

ISBN: 978-1-78864-050-3

British Library Cataloguing in Publication Data. A CIP record for this book can be obtained from the British Library.

Designed and typeset in Palatino by Cinnamon Press. Printed in Poland.

Cover design by Adam Craig © Adam Craig.

Cinnamon Press is represented in the UK by Inpress Ltd and in Wales by the Welsh Books Council.

Acknowledgements

'Breaking Down' appeared in *Acumen*, and 'Fresh' in *Artemis*.

The following were prizewinners in competitions:
'Inclined to Envy Woodlice', Poetry on the Lake; 'Intrigued by Ships', Poems on the Buses, Guernsey; 'Number 25', Grey Hen poetry competition; 'Mothers', Cornwall Contemporary Poetry Competition.

All the poems in the section 'Revisiting the Island', except 'Heart to Heart' and 'Len from Lostwithiel...' were published in a pamphlet, *The Island* (Wayleave Press, Lancaster).

Contents

Seeing Eye

Seeing

Breaking Down

The boom and hiss. What is it
like? Does it suggest the sea: crash
and snaky spreading foam of incessant breakers?
Or a foghorn in a seethe of fog? Or wind
round a stone house, wind through trees?

Lucky to be alive, I think—to have got over
a bad time—survivor of so many years.
But it seems there will never again be
silence.
No getting away—nowhere to turn.

And year by year by year the precious eyes
fail by infinitesimal steps. Birds that are not there
fly across. Shadows hide small dark presences. Something
moves on the periphery. The stretched lens
the furrowed retina grow evasive. Lie.

Why did we trust those five enticing senses
ever? We walk on molecules
held together by faith, see through filters
of self and memory selectively, pretend
what we perceive is real.

Tithonus

Tithonus is everyman—everyone—
but you don't see it until many decades
have passed, many many years,
best part of a million hours. How lucky
you are to have had all these,
all this richness of life! This is what
you craved: more, more.

By now you know how precious
is the arrival of every spring—new leaves,
new acres of promised time—and the arrival
of every new day's light. In love with dawn
though you never realised, longing for it
when you wake from disturbed sleep
too early in the mean small hours.

You took your immortality for granted,
energy expended would be given again,
injuries, exhaustion, foolishness be healed,
each daybreak bring a fresh infinity. Lucky
to have escaped from illness and accident
that took you near the edge. Daily obituaries
have other names attached.

But slowly you come to fear the end of the story—
miles of time to get through, and so much
that doesn't work any more,
sight, hearing, mobility, dwindling—
not the ending that shrinks you to inoffensive insect
but the alternative one, where Dawn,
seeing her human lover lined and wizened,

small ghost still dressed in flesh,
lays him in an anonymous room
that never smells fresh, and locks the door
to stop him wandering, and there,
alone, he babbles endlessly. By then
it would not be death you were afraid of,
if you could remember.

What am I Seeing?

Creeping round the garden, one hand on the white rail,
my mother asks, 'What am I seeing?' How can another
answer? We see through eyes and mind's eye, both. As hard
to look out through someone else as to look in through their eyes
and read them.

My son, colour-blind in one way, my grandson
in another—what would they see if they were with us?
Not that particular pink in the sunset sky. And pedestrians
passing beyond the wall, what do they see, hurrying
with their thoughts and phones?

Once when I was in love the pavement itself seemed luminous
and the suburban street was as vivid as India.
I don't know what my mother can see (registered blind,
slipping into dementia) on this wintry day
in this locked garden.

Afterwards, sipping tea, we talk about seeing things.
Life must be hard, I say, with such limited vision.
'What do you mean?' she asks, looking up
through her useless glasses (not sure, perhaps, who I am)
'I can see perfectly well.'

Ocean City

Intrigued By Ships

because the sea is a foreign country
because it's a door shut on secrets
because it knows no limits
because it would kill you with cold
and starve you with salt
because it steals light and tries to blind you
because if you go far out you are lost

and because they belong to that alien element
because they're islands floating on nowhere
because like swans they seem effortless
because on a grey day they're almost invisible
because they lie in wait
because they swell as they come closer
and closer and shut out the sky
because they bristle with guns, funnels, inexplicable masts
and moving parts
and sometimes approach between wings of water
because they disappear at first light
because they look like nothing earthly

Storm

Because I hadn't expected it, in spite of the night
that roared like being in an aeroplane
and punched the locked doors open, I didn't believe
what I glimpsed through the window's waterfall.

First light was hardly light at all and out of the gloom
great wings of white loomed up and something came at us,
blinded the glass, crashed to the ground and the road
ran whitewater. Again it reared and lunged—

angry cloud, tree of ice, sheeted ghost
and hurled shrapnel of iron and granite. Who knew
the sea hated us so much? It bites the land,
tears the air and breaks, breaks, breaks.

Poppies on the Hoe

I've seen a wave like this
coming at me tall as a house
in that storm, but white not red.

This is a wave of blood, metal, air
rising out of the ground like a resurrection.
But there aren't enough poppies.

7,000 lost at sea in the first war,
16,000 in the second. The wave,
enmeshed, seems to lunge at the sea,

grey endless ocean behind the war memorial,
as if longing to be reunited,
to take flight from its land anchorage.

Poppies at the base of the wave
grow from stone, outliers in ones
and small groups from grass,

each one different in its uniform —
taller, shorter, straight or bending,
with its own disposition of petals

which lack the fragility, the thinness
of living ones. The wind can't move them,
they are set, ceramic, hardened to immortality.

Wave — a poppy sculpture displayed on Plymouth Hoe

Blight City

My shock, when I turned in that high place:
the grassy plateau with sheep and trees,
ocean view framed by overhanging leaves,
pyramid-island in the bay—turned,
wandered a little way, inland as I thought,
and there—

my amateurish picture tries to show you—
a sad blue eye of water at the centre, no mystic pool
but an unexpected glimpse of estuary
and on its further shore, crammed, endless,
the city, heaped and glittering,
a chaos

of pale buildings stuck in the grime of their shadows,
row on row like tideline above tideline of plastic rubbish.
And see what they've done to the sky! Top of the picture's
clear blue, then colourless, then it turns murky—
greyish? brownish? Look what we've done
to the air!

Roy

He's waiting for the girl to come and paint him
(old age mainly made up of waiting) and she's
a woman not a girl, though there's something
forever young about her. A local girl
that's how he thinks of her, but she's good,
she's had exhibitions all over. She does
seascapes and still lifes but he likes the portraits best,
portraits of people he knows from the twin villages.

While he waits he watches the far-off yachts
as they potter and pirouette on the blue water.
Nearest thing to flying for us wingless insects,
he thinks. That boat there, its white sails firm
with the pressure of light, hardly stirs the sea's surface—
its pale reflection swims fishlike beside it. Once
it was his hands, his mind working with wind and water.

He misses that companionship, housebound now
so that the real world, cut off by glass, seems shrunk
to a television fiction. But here she comes,
an inrush of life with her untidiness and laughter,
unpacks paints, palette, brushes, rags, opens out her easel—
embarrassed apologies—but he's cheered by the breeze of her,
by the yellow-ochre gush of sand on to the carpet.
If he can't get to the beach, she's brought the beach in!

On the Buses

1. From the Bus Stop

A building forever in the process of becoming.
For years, nothing. Plans argued over.
Then, a hole. An un-building.

At last the meccano construction: steel girders
rise into the air. Day after week after month
we gaze at it from the bus stop. It's clamorous —

metal on metal's magnified finger-nail-down-blackboard screech.
Grunts and groans from the great crane. Anonymous
thuds and crashes. A construction necessary

for the watchers waiting for the late-arriving bus.
Come out early in case… Again and again disappointed.
Otherwise there is only the somnolent restaurant,

the row of white buildings with their balconies,
turrets and sightless windows; the large sky,
Mediterranean blue today

and the enormous sea — thrilling to visitors,
overfamiliar to us. Yes, there are complex blues,
stony or slumbrous greys, whitecaps perhaps, white edges,

and the light: lines of it, pools of it, sparkle and glare.
Sometimes burning snow all the way to the headland.
But what use is beauty to our stalled

mornings, our unfulfilled longing
for the miniature bus to appear
like a mirage on the distant hill?

2. Number 25

Circle, oblong, ellipse—it's a round and round route
like the seasons, like the years of which we have seen
so many, but today we're not asking
How many more? we're living in the sunny now.
The 9.43's the first we can travel on
free with our passes—shore to shops and back to the beginning.

They all know each other (I'm the stranger).
Westcountry voices greet each slow new arrival:
John from Rusty Anchor, Geraldine from the corner flats
and after St. Andrew's school, the woman with white hair
neat on her shoulders, shadowed by her husband.
Her speech is glossolalia. He never hushes her.

And the bus is full of chatter—a flock of birds.
The journey itself is destination. Later
there'll be new pleasures: market, post office—
but for the moment this is enough. If the driver's early
at Lockyer Street he'll halt the ticking bus
and we'll settle ourselves to enjoy the interlude.

An hour at the shops and we're back to savour the end
of the outing. Past the bombed church, up to the citadel—
no need of phones or electronic distractions.
The high point of the drive is here—now—as we round the curve
and head south downhill and the whole huge sea
opens its plain of light in front of us.

3. Journey to the Centre of my Head

To the right, grey river disappears into mist
upcountry. To the left, its outflow to the sea
seems blocked.

After the bridge we leave the familiar highway.
Now it's all green, trees, many many, perhaps millions
in early-summer leaves,

but no light in them, no gold, no shadow, as if
we're travelling deeper and deeper in
to a forest filled with fog.

Here, though, trees thin, stand singly. Each has its shape—
its gestures—as if the disposition of its outstretched arms
were speaking to us

but I know it's not. Trees have their own objectives,
indifferent to ours. Mist thickens. Now we jerk to an abrupt
stop. A sign says

No Man's Land. The irregular rocking of the bus
resumes. And stops again. Another sign: Great Tree.
No-one gets off.

Then finally the old road steep down dark under
more arching branches. Glimmer of water. Shall we find
our destination down there?

Gone Away?

The house is silent. I am away this weekend
otherwise I would hear the hiss in my head
that sounds like permanent rain and the muffled padding
of my sheepskin slippers across the carpets.

Today the furniture can relax into its own coolness
or bask undisturbed in the sheets of sun which shift
imperceptibly second by second. The houseplants
are getting on with their own affairs — the leaves

of the Christmas plant changing colour pixel by pixel,
the old stub of a geranium flaunting its fiery flag.
Left to themselves the rooms have a settled contentment,
shut windows their defence against disturbance.

The house is enjoying its privacy. But, I tell it
from across the county boundary, you are a child
who needs tending. The green and red plants will be
the first things to wither without me. That stale smell

will take over if I leave your rooms for long.
Mould will colonise the kitchen. Imagine
the bowl of fruit in its slow alterations of decay.
And without me, what will be your reason for existing?

The House with the Golden Windows

Sometimes the headland across the water is erased
by sea-mist. Often afternoons are cloudy, so
you might never have seen, at the end of the day,
the panes of that small house right on the top

of the opposite promontory shine like suns.
If you did, you would want to go there, find that bright place,
but how, with no boat to carry you over
and the web of roads confused by spurs and inlets

in the cup of the great bay? And if you did set out,
swam the mile of blackness then climbed, or drove
through the night, nosing forwards, turning back
from dead ends, seeking out bridges,

if you could get there even in imagination,
you would at last reach a house that looked back
through dark glass, over all that water,
back to where you started from

and—as the sun crept up behind you—
you'd look across to your own diminished
far away house and all its familiar windows
would turn to burning gold.

Hortus Conclusus

Small, secret, swaddled in high walls,
the only garden here, between two terraces
where the road abruptly bends away.

Not quite a triangle, more a trapezium:
rear wall short as if to cheat the eye
with false perspective hinting distance,

front wall you can't see over from the pavement.
Sides are the blank cream end
of the Victorian terrace, the grey windowed side

of the last Edwardian house.
A gull could look in, or the naval helicopters
that overfly the Sound.

I only know a garden's there
by the leafy tops of shrubs, low trees
teasingly glimpsed above the coping stones.

Hidden, invisible, but necessary. Surrounding
these tall houses: tarmac of the street,
paving slabs, granite cobbles in the service lane,

asphalted yards for parking. And out there
beyond the road and iron railings,
the cold salt desert of the sea.

Night Light

Waking, then wideawake, at two or three or four.
What woke me? Was it a noise in the alleyway
or only the whirling in my brain: flickers
and darts and runs of light—neurons and pathways?

Shall I lie there and try to sleep? Or get up and walk?
No need to switch on lamp or torch here
at the edge of the city where nights are lit.
Draw back the blinds and look over the bay:

marine lights, red, green, white, blue, flashing in patterns
of colour and dark, lights mirrored to long tails
on water calm but not quite flat—distorting glass—
and there! the travelling lights of a small craft, silent.

No moving car, no footfall in the lamplit street.
Hard to make out stars above. Walk through the quiet rooms,
(hall's moss-soft carpet, the kitchen one like woollen pebbles)
to the landward view: security lights, parked cars, dim house-backs

from the next road north. And by the high hedge
where flocks of sparrows sleep, the one gold window,
always alight all night: a softened glow,
a hint of smaller, whiter gleam behind.

Uncurtained, every night illuminated
from dusk to breakfast-time, then black
when it looks out on daylight from its terrace
of divided houses—rooms and flats.

Who is it there who never sleeps? Someone ill or dying,
who never moves and never comes to look out past parked cars
over the hedge of sleeping birds towards me
standing invisible in my dark kitchen?

Eye

The Cutting of the Eye

As if from the bottom of a well, looking up
at a white sun. Or no—because the swirling
element's pale blue—more

as if a small fish or glassy shrimp
looked up through shallow sea on a sunny day—
beside the island, perhaps.

Shall I be left forever with a tremble
at the edge of vision, more blueness
in the colours of the world?

I'm lying utterly still—not relaxed
like a drowned man but rigid,
a willed stillness in every muscle

and above me a widening ripple-ring
of blue as if a shining tunnel
was opening up ahead.

New Eye

Nothing is simple—
no plain surface. Even the cobbles in the lane
are veined and spotted. That dark bush
I never knew was variegated holly.
Grey roofs are small square tiles, that brown one
rounded shingles. The concrete slab is a glued beach.

Nothing is single
but a collection of parts—those trees
with their speaking shapes no more than
hosts of leaves huddled together.
Your hair not a singular thing but hairs
various in colour and direction.

The world is silted
with grime—the cobbled alley black-edged,
the autumn leaves freckled with death. Inside the house
skirtings furred with dust, the shadow
on that window a million dots of dirt
brought by the rain that should have washed us clean.

The Ruined Women

I'm not speaking of reputation
but of skin.
Look at the faces, the crumpled necks
of these nicely-dressed women
sitting here
in the poetry workshop. Look
at that one's ruched back-of-the-hand.

The intelligent eyes are underscored,
foreheads corrugated, cheeks
cross-hatched as if by cat's-paw breezes.
The face in the mirrored pillar
is mine. I'm shocked by it.
What happened
on the night of the eye-operation?

I have no memory of being taken
into the magic hill. Of the drought, heat,
struggle, terror that have marked me.
I aged ten years—more—in that one night.
When I came back no-one had missed me,
but the world was blighted
by my seeing.

Mismatched

By day the new eye wins out every time,
presents a world I never knew: a brave
new world, or one that's scuffed and spotted?
Wonderful to see so far, to see the opposite shore,
draw distance close, almost, you think, to see beyond
the horizon, to see the future coming in like weather.

At night the old eye, the poor, sore one,
gets its revenge. Streetlamps, headlights, traffic-lights—
the new eye sees as hard stars, pinpricks—
are lost in great blurred auras, red, green, orange,
yellow and white, so that the city seems to be
a maze of colours cast by a stained-glass window.

Revisiting The Island

Herring Gulls over Little Island

It's the flight we envy   wings   the third dimension
the spaciousness of sky.   These birds seem to be in the air
because they can   half over land   half over sea.
They're not diving for fish   not visiting
nests on the brown rocks   apparently aimless.

Wings stiff and almost still   just the tiniest
dips and adjustments   sometimes a few flaps and then
they slide   as if across ice   slither
as if down snow-slopes.   Air is their plaything
they ride it   balance on it motionless.

From the front   each bird's a splayed M.   From above
from below   almost flat   light as a balsa-wood model.
From the side it's an arrow   a pointed missile
pale straight line from beak to streamlined tail
and taut tucked legs.   They can fly straight lines

or curves   they can bank   and turn   make it look effortless.
Imagine the cool flow along head neck body
over and under wings.   And as they fly they cry
out   is it from pleasure?   Look at that gull
lying on the wind   and laughing.

Silence and Slow Time

Still after three days I'm struck by the silence.
There's no road here. Tractor's at rest in its shed.
From this end of the island the generator's inaudible.
You wouldn't hear the boatman at the jetty
or on the beach, even if he came.

No flight-path or railway in earshot.
No traffic-hum near or far. No people passing—
no voice, slam of door, clack and slap of shoes.
Only that slight hiss in the ear that says I exist,
the background tick of blood, my accumulating moments.

Last night's cloudy moon has brought a weather-change.
Island has shrunk into itself: house, garden,
scribble of trees and blur of water held in a dome of mist.
Thick air, thick silence, not just an absence
of noise, but an enclosing presence.

Not even the sound of the sea against the rocks.
What might I hear in this hush or see in this cloud?
And will there now be quietness in the mind,
will worries that mob and chatter thin to vapour?
I think this is a place where I shall sleep.

Christmas Dinner

Sacramental, you could say,
but perhaps all meals are—
all meals taken together.

Together—all the family:
my children, their spouses,
their children. This will surely be

the only time here on the island
in midwinter, since they live
so scattered over the globe.

Until the last group disembarked,
splashing through freezing surf
from gangplank to sand

this fragile plan
was only a fine dream. The sea
wild, the icy spray

sprinkling a cold baptism
on the astonished baby
in his orange lifejacket.

And the turkey, briefly, left behind
in the boat—the turkey I'd got lost
looking for in nameless lanes.

But here we are—almost a miracle—
eleven of us in this room of lights:
the shining tree, the yule log

with its line of flame.
The huge turkey a golden centrepiece,
the gleam from glass and bottle.

In the darkening afternoon
outside, the excluded
sea and wind prowl round.

Hog-roast

Watching over the pig in its coffin
I can see beyond it that cottage where we stayed —
how many times? — the dark pink roses
over the stone wall, ivy and belladonna,
and beside the battered house a dead tree
whitish against the shadows.

Heat on my face and chest — at first I think
it's from the orange sun preparing to sink
into the sycamore wood, but no, I can see
the warmth rising against my shirt, not quite
like smoke or a pattern of light and shade,
more of a tremor in the air.

I peer through the glass panels in the roof
of the steel box. The pig's long back, scored and furrowed —
its rounded hillocks and slopes like the Cornish landscape —
is browning and shining between two rows
of little flames, which must be kept burning
despite the breeze from behind me,

from the blank plain of the sea, the cloudless sky.
No human sound, but there is music
for the vigil, ghost-voices of invisible birds —
a pigeon's exhausted complaint,
a chanting of gulls dulled by distance,
a sudden long soprano cry.

Heart to Heart

Removed from the knotted plastic bag
it's pear-shaped, crimson with a creamy frieze

and shiny. Call it art-object,
heart of gold, almost a Fabergé egg.

Call it emblem or metaphor,
flaming heart, symbol of charity.

Life-gift. Anaemia bleaches me.
This heart's blood will give me vigour.

In the small hours I listen to
the steady metronome—heart of darkness.

I look at the heart, reluctant
to cut—heart-break—to lay open

the intricate halls and heart-strings,
but I accept what is offered

and prepare now for the ceremonious
heart-warming with herbs, spices and wine.

Grace to the pig to whom I fed
apples under the tamarisk.

Thou Watchest the Last Oozings,
Hours by Hours

It has stood for weeks now. I thought it had stopped —
jar not quite full — but no, the bronze
level has crept up. Over the glass opening
the bag hangs pendulous from its red tripod
on the windowsill. Nothing's synthesised,
synthetic, changed by human hand —

it's the bees' work, the bees that gather
sweetness from island flowers in garden
field and wood. The white bag,
yellowed at its base, holds crumpled honeycomb.
And look! against the pane a shining drop
slower than rain, more viscous, nipple of light.

The day waits for it. Like raindrops will it swell,
change shape? Don't touch! Don't hurry it
with sticky fingers — it needs stillness.
The tiny hemisphere lengthens, drinks more sunlight.
Now it's an hourglass telling slow time, and now
comes the reluctant severance, like a sigh.

And at once the drop's lost in the dark pool
leaving behind a brief white stalactite
to rise back into a new small bead of gleam.

Len from Lostwithiel Will Collect Them at the West Quay

That marauding mallard drake blew
in on the wind and wouldn't leave
the island ducks alone. Driven
off, back he came

back he came. Now twelve dark ducklings,
half-fledged, must emigrate ashore.
The young woman brings a metal
cage and sprinkles

food pellets. Ducks approach, withdraw,
run round the outside. A young one
tiptoes in, and out. Finally
all the ducklings

are in, door slammed, but the mother,
the black Indian Runner, hops
and dances around the crate, calls
out to her brood

and their small voices answer her
in a choir of alarm. The two
women try cornering her but
no, she flutters

away squawking, and the plaintive
chorus grows louder. At last she's
caught in a hug, bundled inside.
The awkward cage

must be carried now, one woman
padding backwards down the narrow
path and the small flight of steps with
a turn in it

down to the jetty where the boat
rocks uneasily on the sea.
The boatman and his companion
embark the crate

and set off over blue water
through the blue air to the distant
mainland, the ducks' complaint slowly
dissipating.

Rough

Woke at five to a muted booming—wind
drumming on the thick-walled house and water
smashing itself on the shore. Hard to make out
much through the salted glass.

A phone call—there's no going to the mainland
today. The harbour bar impassable—wind in the east
(which the gulls on their rocks expected yesterday
facing Rame Head instead of Talland).

There's fish in the freezer (boatman's gift), tomatoes
reddening in the greenhouse, plenty of windfalls
for the pigs. Shame the ducks have stopped laying
and hens hide their nests in the wood.

I unpack my packed bag, put on the kettle,
hope the gas will last. The beamed rooms
have a look of strangeness as if containing,
as well as me, my anticipated absence.

How long, how long? The islanders were marooned
three weeks last winter. The clock in the hall has stopped
and I don't know how to get it going.
I wonder—can time move on without it?

Crossing

The granite steps on the west quay—what delightful
solidity. A surface that stays still.

It was a tough crossing—the tip of the mast
with its twin flags, Cornwall and UKIP, drawing a wide arc

on the blurred air. Fresh water pelted us
from above, salt water from below—

sea black as winter and all on the move in shifting
white-tipped peaks and canyons. Boat rolling and dipping

and the island fading behind us, mist
on mist, paler and smaller and then   not there.

Truth And Fiction

And Did those Feet?

Unlikely, but who knows?
The island is a page that has been written on,
erased, rewritten and overwritten again and again,
now scarcely legible. The all-too-brief excavation
produced some solid evidence (stone, bone, potsherd)

but the history is full of gaps and guesswork.
No reference in Domesday, a few
mentions in documents and travellers' tales,
an inscribed list of chaplains in a church.
Other information is lost—

records destroyed in fire and war.
On the Armada map the small island is topped
with a vanished chapel or monastery—
sometimes inhabited, sometimes, it seems, abandoned.
Perhaps a place of pilgrimage.

And perhaps because it was a holy site someone dreamt up
the legend of the Christ-child left to play
alone on the green hill by his great-uncle
the travelling merchant Joseph of Arimathea.
It could conceivably be true

but probably not. After the monks, the smugglers—
do you imagine them romantic, swashbuckling?
Or was it just the Finns and Hoopers on the cliffs
in the mist and dark, middlemen running their business,
hauling up contraband to store under the barn?

Conjecture, much of the story. There are
sea-hollowed caves on the west side, frescoed
with coloured algae. But those rumours of tunnels
to the mainland, the whole island riddled
like honeycomb with caves, are fantasies.

And what of the crumbling treasure-map
with X marking the spot, sent by a mythical
clergyman from Cumbria? Nothing was found
but a stone. The island remains silent. The seabirds,
its oldest inhabitants, speak an alien language.

Truth and Fiction

I'll start with the tattered book, because it's real,
solid—the look, the feel, the weight, the smell—
a breaching whale on the leather-effect cover,
a cloud of silver spray, an upturned boat
and drowning men.

Heft it—be careful, the century has broken it:
True Tales for my Grandsons. The prologue begins:
The love of truth is a charm in human nature.
My grandfather showed us it, told us he was
one of the grandsons.

My mother died believing it, passed the book on to me.
But now we have Google and my son's research.
Falling out of any belief is sad, but perhaps
a family legend can't be called a lie—it's more
a kind of wishful thinking.

Our alleged ancestor, that fairly eminent
Victorian: explorer, popular hero
(in spite of the questionable second wife)
had a too-common name, spoor hard to follow.
Some descendants can

be traced through the web's complexities,
but they're strangers. How could they have lost us?
But how could my grandfather, that principled,
godfearing man, have given us, for a truth,
something that's not?

The faded book with its gilt-edged pages
seems like a solid piece of evidence. But no.
Who now can vouch for the truth of the tall stories,
the author dead for more than a hundred years?
Grandfather, dead half a century,

can't say if someone told him the tale of the famous
forebear, if he believed it, or perhaps invented it—
old man in an armchair in a South London suburb
travelling in his mind across the world
and to and fro in time.

On Lasseter Highway

Red dust. Grey scrub. Bleached grass. And heat.
Mile after mile beside the road. Occasional squat trees
with hairlike foliage, low ridges like crinkles in quilts,
white stones on the redness, a bird, a dried-up
river-bed.

The air-conditioned coach slides us along his highway
across the burning land. No, not on fire, though—look!
There and there in the jumped-up scrub: charcoal
among tussocks, little black trees, dead as the ghost-towns
we don't go to.

The guide's words flow through the monotony
like a distant broadcast. My son says a lot of it's fiction—
but I'm hooked. Was he hero or con-man? That claim—
truth or post-truth? Well, we all have dreams.
Sometimes they kill us.

What did he believe, and when? How far is memory
to be trusted? Like a holy vision, his reef of gold.
Thirty years later he still spoke of it, eyes looking
not at but through his listeners. At first their gaze, too,
slid away.

Later they wanted to believe as he did, dreamers
playing the lottery, with more to lose than money.
Hour after hour, now, we cross the desert landscape—
the hot orange of sunlight through eyelids.
Day after day,

year after year after decade for him. Heat-bitten,
desiccated, his body destroyed itself towards his goal.
On a huge hill, (yes, low red mountains)
cragged and steep, Truth stands, and hee that will
reach her must give his life.

Yet people called him charlatan, eccentric, mad. Something
had shone for him (but him only). When even
the dingo-shooter doubted him and left, the camels ran away,
the indigenous people who rescued him
took offence and went,

he was alone in that endless place: red grit, grey shrubs,
deadness and heat, with his scrawled maps of nowhere,
the diary he buried—dying words to his wife: *What good a reef
worth millions? I'd give it all for a loaf of bread!* Or water.
Water.

H B Lasseter: 1880-1931. Lasseter Highway: Northern Territory, Australia

A Visit to the Immigration Museum

Pictures of ships. I imagine their white sails
like flocks of wings blown by the wind out of our harbour
out of Plymouth Sound to the open sea across the world.

A grey plaque on a grey wall in the Barbican:
Charlotte and *Friendship* set out from there
more than two hundred years ago.

Below-decks no beauty, each ship holding
a hundred criminals. Eight months of rats,
lice, bedbugs, cockroaches, fleas and stink.

Charlotte my grandmother lost her brother
to Australia — 1910? 1920?
Never saw him again. (His voyage made in forty days

and nights on an Aberdeen Line steamship.)
My sons too have gone to their far continents,
not carried by lovely squalid sailing ships,

or steamers with yellow funnels breathing heat,
but through the sky in silver, propelled by
a sense of adventure, chance-met brides.

With some expense of money and spirit
I can visit, along with all those other
grey-haired parents wondering how much longer,

can land in January summer, stroll
in white cotton beside the shining skyscrapers
to the museum in Flinders Street

and learn about the breaking of families.
Convicts of the First Fleet — first flood to wash up
on this shore to start the new nation.

After them wave on wave of arrivals
endless as ocean, millions of scattered souls
spun round the globe on currents of air and water.

Remembering The Dale

Light from Dead Years

Only in dreams now, but the sleeping mind remembers
driving westward too eager for home, meeting
that curve of ice, astonished to find I'm facing
backwards. But the road's deserted.

Down there a huddled village glitters
in the palm of the hills, then night
floods back, trees black, black river. Healaugh,
Low Row, Gunnerside brief interruptions.

Then climb towards the sky. I know each bend,
each gearchange. Lonely farms are dark.
No streetlights and no wandering sheep
with green flames in their eyes.

Pray not to wake. At last I reach that ledge
on the abrupt hill. Headlamps go off, the engine ticks.
I'm out and looking up. All the wide silence overhead
is lit with thousands, millions of icy stars.

The Hamlet

From the opposite slope it seems a poor small thing,
sprinkle of freckles on the greenness—
five cottages, two barns and a cowshed
and all that bare
land and all that air.

Arduously, doggedly I chase
my house back through the censuses—
all houses here seemingly named the same
the rest of the address
anyone's guess.

Street name: none. Village: now this, now that.
Town: too far away to count. Hide-and-seek hamlet—
now you see it, now you're stuck.
But look round you—it's here, rooted, here
for a thousand years

ever since the norseman kept his cattle
on this plateau, served by the same good spring
now piping water to the houses
(rough pasture above, hay meadows below)
which, a hundred years ago

were alive with children. When I first came:
one small family, two farmers and me. When I left
I was single at the top, lone gamekeeper downhill. A quiet place
slow as a tree in its dying back,
old stones sinking to bedrock.

That Hillside

We came 'over the mountain' in drizzle. I joked
that the sun always shone in Swaledale,
because, in a sense, it did.
And as we came over the brow and nosed down
round the right-angled bend by the millennium cairn,
the greyness did yellow a bit and brighten.

And when we got down to the valley floor,
the dale road (so familiar), I looked up to my hillside
and it was rainbow. Not with a semicircle
arching over it. Colour was laid along the slope.
A broad band of red at the top, like fire.
A stripe of gold. Shading to blue above the river.

The hillside
was transfixed, touched with glory. Trees
barely in bud and drystone walls and isolated farms,
acres of grass, seen through the strangeness.
That was my house, my hill lived on and walked on
in all weathers for all those years,
but never in the body of a rainbow.

While the Sun Shines

A field of grass, dense and tall
and still so many flowers: buttercup daisy stitchwort
yellow-rattle eyebright

hawkbit clover late pignut and early yarrow
last purple-and-white cranesbill
sorrel and plantain

and grasses, some feathery, some furry
and some like ears of thin green wheat—
a secret humming world.

Seven meadows from river to village.
We walk through all the stages of hay
though not in order.

The second's a shorn plain, sand-cloured, arid
as the flagstone path across it. Oystercatchers peck
among the stubble.

But the third field's full of work: men,
tractors, trailers. All the rowed-up hay squeezed
into squared bales

surprisingly greener than when it lay scattered.
Saddest is the next meadow, where what's lying
is still grass, still with a shine,

neatly laid out in flat swathes. Among the sappy stems
flowers for their own funerals—white and glossy yellow
that still reflects the sun.

Past the stone stile there's another grumbling tractor
turning the paler hay—whiffling, Paul called it, tossing
the dry stalks over

in clouds of intoxicating scent, the field path
under a light covering that creaks and gives as you pass
like new dry snow;

though the turned hay in the next field, left
to settle since yesterday, has been booted aside
from the track

and all that's left for your feet is a soft
powder fallen to earth from the grey
flowers of grass.

How quickly it comes back from the dead, the green aftermath,
like the rise on the back of an old ewe whose fleece
hangs off in shreds.

Here in the last field the flimsy hopeful grass
hurries to live again. Again and again springs up
to be mown down.

Fog in the Dale

Yes, you could see it as a lid, a wall
to wall you in, lens of cloud on your eye,
opaque atmosphere hard to breathe, a hill
of cold upended in your valley. But go
out into it, feel its gentle moisture stroke
your skin. Mist makes the everyday mysterious.
Inhale its cool—you can—a soothing smoke
and look and dream: everything's its own ghost.
Grass-flowers, heavy with dew, are asphodel,
invisible water sings to the shadows of the dead.
A clock from nowhere strikes its timeless bell
and a sudden tree's a giant thinking head.
Then you must climb. Keep climbing. Believe you'll be born again
to stand on a sheepskin floor in the dazzle of the sun.

Swaledale Snow

I miss the place. But life was hard when it snowed.
You watched for it: forecast, source of the wind,
look of the sky. You'd move the car before the road
got choked — the steep slope, that perilous bend.
Oil-tankers couldn't reach you, so no heat
except the fire. No water if the spring froze.
The phone-line always failed. Even to walk out
was tricky on the underlay of ice.

Difficult but beautiful. If snow is white,
white was a gamut of colours: violet, green,
blue; gold and silver set with chips of light;
rosy at sunset, then indigo. It was a tide
rising to drown the walls, drown the past, to hide
the dark and make the rough smooth, a mirror for the moon.

Mothers

The rat slid softly under the gate—the stone step
hollowed by centuries of footfall. A mother perhaps,
scuttling to forage for her brood.
There were

rats about that year, and the next.
(Get rid of them before the children come!) I blamed
Ronnie's barn downhill. I'd have to call in Richard
and his blue poison.

The log-store was half full with Cocker John's
spruce—not much needed that spring. One day
the wood was chirping. If I hid and waited
two blackbirds came

taking turns, swooping their clean curves to the low entrance.
And in the dimness, on a cut log
a palisade of nest, small squeakings.
Three mornings later

the browner bird was there in the yard
alone. Hopping, fluttering, crying out
in a hoarse voice. All that day and all the next.
Maybe all night—

I kept away. But when, in the end, I looked:
no nest, no tiny open beaks. The log's yellow circle
swept bare, and the mother bird still on the flagstones
unafraid,

making that ugly noise—like the dry-throated calling
of the ewes that clustered on the track in summer
above the farm where their lost lambs
had last been sighted.

Missing

Last year we heard it first in the yellow
evening light beside the roofless chapel
on the hill—the two clear notes floating
on empty air across the valley

from Kearton's Wood. Year after year I'd heard
one there, and another like an echo
further up, from the gill at Rash.
Now I walk westward, listening

to the far side of the dale, but—
nothing. There's the lapwing's wiry cry,
curlew's bubbling halloo, lark higher and higher
and the small songbirds in the farmer's trees

but not the cuckoo's monotonous couplet.
Invisible bird, that abandons its child,
free spirit at all costs—what have we done
to it? Why has it not come back?

Double Vision

That green ridge over the quiet valley
is doubled, one hill above the other. If one
is false, can either be relied on?

And this hay-meadow, next to be cut,
bright with buttercups, pignut, cranesbill,
exists twice over,

the upper, floating field a little mistier,
as if the memory of it—all that will be left
after the mowing

when the living beauty is erased,
razed to the ground—
is hovering here already.

On the way home the train alongside ours
is split, its doppelgänger on its roof
like a fatal derailment.

When I come back next year
let me see single, so that I can lift up
my eyes to the hills

and believe in their solidity—
that they will go on being here
after I've gone.

Flora and Fauna

'Monet is just an eye'

Cezanne

My eye has changed the world. What's real—the before or after?
Or neither? I liked the eroded silhouette
of the fort far out to sea, the vanishings
and materialisations of big ships—pale dark green grey,
the misty headland sometimes more present sometimes less,
believed my friends and I were hardly touched by time.

Words had grown mottled, indistinct—sometimes my brain
guessed strange messages. Now suddenly the letters
turn black, admonitory. I see the city
across the water edged and angular
in the harsh sea-light, see myself a hag,
a crone, and my cheerfulness about myself is lost.

I comfort myself with pictures—these waterlilies,
the shifting shapes of a liquid surface. Monet looked out
from his near-blindness, saw the world as an evolving place,
in colours we might not have expected. He trusted
his cataract-vision to show a kind of truth.
Now I must learn to trust clarity.

Fresh

As this winter ends I'm amazed by the intricacy of trees.
Before, I might have likened their naked crowns to lace,
but now I see them as if I were the lacemaker
and every thread, knot, loop had left its print
and numbness on my fingertips.

Now it's every several twig I marvel at, how the tree
has a wholeness, a precise perimeter shape
you could draw round its extremities—and every budding twig
contributes to the main idea. Inside the shape—say
club, spade, disc, obelisk or cloud—

such a complexity it would take hours, days even,
to unravel. And when spring starts I might have said, once,
the trees were hazed with green. But no:
spotted, speckled, sprinkled with individual
greennesses as buds change size, shape, colour

until they're not buds, each is a tiny leaf or cluster
folded or scrolled, or else they're petals—
ruffles and frills in such abundance that I stand
like an idiot staring up, wondering
how branches can bear such burdens of excess.

In her 75th Year She Discovers Daisies

and they're everywhere! In San Sebastian Square
the cherry-blossom is long gone, but now
a confetti of daisies whitens the ground
under the trees.

That small triangle of lawn by the flats
is thickly drifted with daisies standing proud
of the grass as if fallen softly
down from sky.

When she walks round the bay the low wall
that holds the Hoe back from the road
presents them at eye-height for her scrutiny.
If you pick them

they feel like feathers, like nothing, weightless
in the hand. It's hard to count the almost translucent
thin straight petals—forty perhaps?
—their narrow-arch tips

and their undersides, not always but often,
a surprise of crimson. And the flower's centre
isn't flat but domed—pincushion set with a hundred
yellow pinheads.

In damp and dusk the daisies curl into themselves
but in the morning sun they open towards the east
and all day track the source of life and heat
as if gazing after a lover.

Inclined to Envy Woodlice

who die neatly, causing no trouble, corpses
pleasant as the stiff covers of buds;

who have never resented butterflies
or even beetles, being contented.

Marsupial, they keep their babies close,
a tranquil love-in-action,

asking only to be allowed to serve
the fertile earth until such time

as they themselves are patched into its quilt
of shreds and scraps, of weeds and leaf-lace.

In the Council Offices

Abseiling down the scuffed white wall, a tiny spider.
The floor is empty. I have arrived early
to report my lost bus pass. Soon there will be
crowds of careless feet. I am concerned
but can't communicate. The shopping precinct
outside would be no safer for it.

Spider sets off across the floorboards. Stops.
He who hesitates is lost, I tell it silently.
It carries on to a strip of carpet, pauses
among dark marks. I fear it will become one.
Two pairs of shoes approach, miss it by inches.
It moves again towards a bench, set oddly
on a reflective plinth. Stops to consider.

Can spiders see in mirrors? Might it, territorial,
perceive an enemy? It turns and trots
alongside the glassy wall, in tandem with
what now seems like an imaginary friend.
But turns again. The two dots part, step out
into their short and lonely future.

Death of a Tree

1. Prayer For A Eucalyptus In Seven Haikus

Death climbs up the tree,
up the skeletal branches
to the topmost twigs—

they curve with the wind
as if only there, that high,
is air breathable.

The last tree standing
between the sea's wilderness
and the stone city:

Is it dead? she asked.
For days I watch the slight crest
for a thickening,

a curdling of air,
a clotting—are those new leaves
or very small birds?

See how that grey cloud
passing behind the branches
fills them with silver!

Oh resurrection—
how hungrily we long for
life from dying wood.

2. Leaning Tree

Torn between felling it and letting be. Yes
it is dead. It could fall. But it's the only tree
seen from our windows on this shore (I miss
green—those bare hills, grass with its shimmer of wet)

though for these five years the eucalyptus
has brought forth very little green—just the odd puff,
quiff, crest or plume to scatter its rounded leaves
at any season, until those February storms,

salt winds that stripped the last twigs bare.
From the back, north, it's a sad sight: lopped, knobbly,
a mutilated skeleton black as if charred.
Here amputated below the elbow,

there splintered to a spike.
The main tree must have died before I came
and what my window showed was the one live
branch still leafing in patches.

From where I sit to read, the tall window
frames the tree's south side precisely—
a complicated tangle of curling arms,
some of them seeming to hug the dead trunk

and its encroaching ivy.
But birds still use it as a singing post.
Sometimes there's a squirrel in it, once a cat,
and colonies of invisible insects.

Sunlight makes the dry and peeling bark
shine and the last fine twigs,
still stretching up—reaching when hope is gone—
look like a crown of copper wire.

3. Shrinking

He wants it felled (parks his car underneath.)
In a storm it sways. The neighbours planted it—
a sapling—now three storeys high. It grew
like a reverse river-system, smaller and smaller
tributaries stretching to sip the air, dry now—
fine twigs, thick branches deader than Lazarus.

The tall thin window needs it. I thought it would go,
when it went, all of a piece—one day a sudden lack
where it had filtered the view of neighbour buildings
for all my time here. But now like something monstrous,
a shock in the early mist, there's a grey man
in the grey tree, legs and arms extra branches.

Later when the sun comes out I see one side's shorn.
Two brightnesses colour the dull and peeling trunk—
sunlit ivy aspiring upwards and a yellow wound,
more of them when I look up from the yard.
Bent limbs piled in a corner.
If I move my chair to the left I shall hardly notice.

4. Jacob's Ladder

Blake painted the angels in long white dresses
on a pale staircase loosely spiralling,

but this ladder's like a crooked totem—a pole
with little stubby steps, prongs left from the amputations.

Angels today are small winged creatures, dark not bright,
though deft of movement. First a small flock,

then a single—how does it move upwards,
effortless and unruffled, from spur to spur?

The top of the dead trunk, where the crown was,
is a flat platform, a sliced-clean surface.

Like an updraught of air the creature's suddenly
up there. And sings. But it's not music

as we understand it, self-consciously constructed.
The being opens itself and the sounds leave it.

Beautiful sounds, but an alien vocabulary.
The creature intends no message to me.

Behind my window I must seem to it

the picture of a person on a screen, not actual.

Sparrows

More than just one family, surely. I counted
twenty of them on the telephone wires
chattering at the blackbird on their
tree. They enjoy the dead tree, don't grieve

for its lost branches, its never-returning leaves.
It's not ugly to them, not a waste of space
or a bone of contention—it's a playground,
a small world of delight. But can we say

'enjoy', 'delight'? Can we call the small flock
happy, merry even? We can only say
how we would feel if we could jump,
flutter, twitter up there, discovering

the various forks and levels over and over.
The sparrows are small, light, agile, same colour
as the cracked and faded wood of the crooked trunk,
the side-spurs, the sawn-flat top.

Beside the tree the old shed has turned into a bush,
a huge fuzz of ivy hiding their nests,
and now while the topmost vertical stems sway and shine
in the wind, the birds perch on them bouncing and swinging.

Seeing Eye

Layered

Don't trust your fine sight too far, your perspicacity,
she thinks as she blanches and flakes the almonds, restoring
the white of the starry flower, the ice-crystal shine
of the blossoming tree.

Putting the biscuits in the oven, she tells herself
eyes only see the outsides of things. After blossom
and green spearhead leaves, the fruit of the almond,
the frosted green plush,

is still not the nub of it. (Oven begins to send out
a warm sweetness.) The almond's green fruit
is not like a velvet-skinned peach. Flesh dries and splits
to reveal the last container.

Inside is where you find the truth. Same as with people?
(She glances through the window—has his car come back?)
Behind the face the skull, inside the skull the brain,
locked in the brain its secret thoughts.

Cloud

Look at that huge cumulus above the sea—
purple, hard-edged, definite as a ridge of hills.
It's not, though.

Take off and rise through cloud—it's insubstantial
as morning sea-mist, as haze, the dimming of a thing,
not thing in itself.

Solid-seeming cloud from my front window
with my new pitiless eyesight. But not from the back
through the Edwardian glass.

Evening cloud over the dead tree: blurred outline
of a blur that moves if you move your head.
Shapeshifting vagueness.

The softened vision of my worn-out eyes restored.
Impressionist vision—broken brush-strokes running into each other,
vibration of varied greys.

Here is the movement of light into darkness, time passing,
flicker of day night day night, becoming and dying.
Do I prefer the clear glass

or the glass insisting it's a liquid? Through it, roofs, walls,
spire and tree-stump are decomposing around the edges,
moving towards their dissolution.

Visual Acuity Chart

Final checkup. I can read the line that says
I'm fit to drive again. On, on my eyesight goes.
Fit to fly, the consultant says. (Fit to fly—eagle eye.)

I've never seen an eagle in the flesh, but sea-birds
I've often watched. How much do gulls make out,
staring down through the water? At home I watch through glass,

see every stain, every scrap of litter in the street,
the bee on the agapanthus, the ant among dust-grains,
each new-climbed inch of ivy on the tree-trunk,

the numbers on the big grey ships, every line
of light, wind, wake, weed, spillage on the Sound,
each mark, each vein, each wrinkle on my face and hands.

Some of the blemishes I see are surely absent
for others. Is it possible to see too much? I'd settle
for an average world, a softening, a human kindness.